PASSWORD
LOG BOOK

THIS NOTEBOOK BELONGS TO

Name:...

Phone:..

Email:...

Address:...

🌐 Website	
👤 Username	
✉ Email	
🔒 Password	
📝 Note	

🌐 Website	
👤 Username	
✉ Email	
🔒 Password	
📝 Note	

🌐 Website	
👤 Username	
✉ Email	
🔒 Password	
📝 Note	

🌐 Website	
👤 Username	
✉ Email	
🔒 Password	
📝 Note	

Website	
Username	
Email	
Password	
Note	

Website	
Username	
Email	
Password	
Note	

Website	
Username	
Email	
Password	
Note	

Website	
Username	
Email	
Password	
Note	

Website	
Username	
Email	
Password	
Note	

Website	
Username	
Email	
Password	
Note	

Website	
Username	
Email	
Password	
Note	

Website	
Username	
Email	
Password	
Note	

🌐 Website	
👤 Username	
✉ Email	
🔒 Password	
📝 Note	

🌐 Website	
👤 Username	
✉ Email	
🔒 Password	
📝 Note	

🌐 Website	
👤 Username	
✉ Email	
🔒 Password	
📝 Note	

🌐 Website	
👤 Username	
✉ Email	
🔒 Password	
📝 Note	

🌐 Website	
👤 Username	
✉ Email	
🔒 Password	
📝 Note	

🌐 Website	
👤 Username	
✉ Email	
🔒 Password	
📝 Note	

🌐 Website	
👤 Username	
✉ Email	
🔒 Password	
📝 Note	

🌐 Website	
👤 Username	
✉ Email	
🔒 Password	
📝 Note	

🌐 *Website*	
👤 *Username*	
✉ *Email*	
🔒 *Password*	
📝 *Note*	

🌐 *Website*	
👤 *Username*	
✉ *Email*	
🔒 *Password*	
📝 *Note*	

🌐 *Website*	
👤 *Username*	
✉ *Email*	
🔒 *Password*	
📝 *Note*	

🌐 *Website*	
👤 *Username*	
✉ *Email*	
🔒 *Password*	
📝 *Note*	

🌐 Website	
👤 Username	
✉ Email	
🔒 Password	
📝 Note	

🌐 Website	
👤 Username	
✉ Email	
🔒 Password	
📝 Note	

🌐 Website	
👤 Username	
✉ Email	
🔒 Password	
📝 Note	

🌐 Website	
👤 Username	
✉ Email	
🔒 Password	
📝 Note	

🌐 Website	
👤 Username	
✉ Email	
🔒 Password	
📝 Note	

🌐 Website	
👤 Username	
✉ Email	
🔒 Password	
📝 Note	

🌐 Website	
👤 Username	
✉ Email	
🔒 Password	
📝 Note	

🌐 Website	
👤 Username	
✉ Email	
🔒 Password	
📝 Note	

🌐 Website	
👤 Username	
✉ Email	
🔒 Password	
📝 Note	

🌐 Website	
👤 Username	
✉ Email	
🔒 Password	
📝 Note	

🌐 Website	
👤 Username	
✉ Email	
🔒 Password	
📝 Note	

🌐 Website	
👤 Username	
✉ Email	
🔒 Password	
📝 Note	

🌐 Website	
👤 Username	
✉ Email	
🔒 Password	
📝 Note	

🌐 Website	
👤 Username	
✉ Email	
🔒 Password	
📝 Note	

🌐 Website	
👤 Username	
✉ Email	
🔒 Password	
📝 Note	

🌐 Website	
👤 Username	
✉ Email	
🔒 Password	
📝 Note	

🌐 Website	
👤 Username	
✉ Email	
🔒 Password	
📝 Note	

🌐 Website	
👤 Username	
✉ Email	
🔒 Password	
📝 Note	

🌐 Website	
👤 Username	
✉ Email	
🔒 Password	
📝 Note	

🌐 Website	
👤 Username	
✉ Email	
🔒 Password	
📝 Note	

🌐 Website	
👤 Username	
✉ Email	
🔒 Password	
📝 Note	

🌐 Website	
👤 Username	
✉ Email	
🔒 Password	
📝 Note	

🌐 Website	
👤 Username	
✉ Email	
🔒 Password	
📝 Note	

🌐 Website	
👤 Username	
✉ Email	
🔒 Password	
📝 Note	

🌐 Website	
👤 Username	
✉ Email	
🔒 Password	
📝 Note	

🌐 Website	
👤 Username	
✉ Email	
🔒 Password	
📝 Note	

🌐 Website	
👤 Username	
✉ Email	
🔒 Password	
📝 Note	

🌐 Website	
👤 Username	
✉ Email	
🔒 Password	
📝 Note	

🌐 Website	
👤 Username	
✉ Email	
🔒 Password	
📝 Note	

🌐 Website	
👤 Username	
✉ Email	
🔒 Password	
📝 Note	

🌐 Website	
👤 Username	
✉ Email	
🔒 Password	
📝 Note	

🌐 Website	
👤 Username	
✉ Email	
🔒 Password	
📝 Note	

🌐 Website	
👤 Username	
✉ Email	
🔒 Password	
📝 Note	

🌐 Website	
👤 Username	
✉ Email	
🔒 Password	
📝 Note	

🌐 Website	
👤 Username	
✉ Email	
🔒 Password	
📝 Note	

🌐 Website	
👤 Username	
✉ Email	
🔒 Password	
📝 Note	

🌐 Website	
👤 Username	
✉ Email	
🔒 Password	
📝 Note	

🌐 Website	
👤 Username	
✉ Email	
🔒 Password	
📝 Note	

🌐 Website	
👤 Username	
✉ Email	
🔒 Password	
📝 Note	

🌐 Website	
👤 Username	
✉ Email	
🔒 Password	
📝 Note	

🌐 Website	
👤 Username	
✉ Email	
🔒 Password	
📝 Note	

🌐 Website	
👤 Username	
✉ Email	
🔒 Password	
📝 Note	

🌐 Website	
👤 Username	
✉ Email	
🔒 Password	
📝 Note	

🌐 Website	
👤 Username	
✉ Email	
🔒 Password	
📝 Note	

E Password Log Book   Date

🌐 Website	
👤 Username	
✉ Email	
🔒 Password	
📝 Note	

🌐 Website	
👤 Username	
✉ Email	
🔒 Password	
📝 Note	

🌐 Website	
👤 Username	
✉ Email	
🔒 Password	
📝 Note	

🌐 Website	
👤 Username	
✉ Email	
🔒 Password	
📝 Note	

🌐 Website	
👤 Username	
✉ Email	
🔒 Password	
📝 Note	

🌐 Website	
👤 Username	
✉ Email	
🔒 Password	
📝 Note	

🌐 Website	
👤 Username	
✉ Email	
🔒 Password	
📝 Note	

🌐 Website	
👤 Username	
✉ Email	
🔒 Password	
📝 Note	

🌐 Website	
👤 Username	
✉ Email	
🔒 Password	
📝 Note	

🌐 Website	
👤 Username	
✉ Email	
🔒 Password	
📝 Note	

🌐 Website	
👤 Username	
✉ Email	
🔒 Password	
📝 Note	

🌐 Website	
👤 Username	
✉ Email	
🔒 Password	
📝 Note	

🌐 Website	
👤 Username	
✉ Email	
🔒 Password	
📝 Note	

🌐 Website	
👤 Username	
✉ Email	
🔒 Password	
📝 Note	

🌐 Website	
👤 Username	
✉ Email	
🔒 Password	
📝 Note	

🌐 Website	
👤 Username	
✉ Email	
🔒 Password	
📝 Note	

🌐 Website	
👤 Username	
✉ Email	
🔒 Password	
📝 Note	

🌐 Website	
👤 Username	
✉ Email	
🔒 Password	
📝 Note	

🌐 Website	
👤 Username	
✉ Email	
🔒 Password	
📝 Note	

🌐 Website	
👤 Username	
✉ Email	
🔒 Password	
📝 Note	

<table>
<tr><td>F</td><td>Password Log Book</td><td>Date</td></tr>
</table>

🌐 Website	
👤 Username	
✉ Email	
🔒 Password	
📝 Note	

🌐 Website	
👤 Username	
✉ Email	
🔒 Password	
📝 Note	

🌐 Website	
👤 Username	
✉ Email	
🔒 Password	
📝 Note	

🌐 Website	
👤 Username	
✉ Email	
🔒 Password	
📝 Note	

<table>
<tr><td>F</td><td>Password Log Book</td><td>Date</td></tr>
</table>

🌐 Website	
👤 Username	
✉ Email	
🔒 Password	
📝 Note	

🌐 Website	
👤 Username	
✉ Email	
🔒 Password	
📝 Note	

🌐 Website	
👤 Username	
✉ Email	
🔒 Password	
📝 Note	

🌐 Website	
👤 Username	
✉ Email	
🔒 Password	
📝 Note	

🌐 *Website*	
👤 *Username*	
✉ *Email*	
🔒 *Password*	
📝 *Note*	

🌐 *Website*	
👤 *Username*	
✉ *Email*	
🔒 *Password*	
📝 *Note*	

🌐 *Website*	
👤 *Username*	
✉ *Email*	
🔒 *Password*	
📝 *Note*	

🌐 *Website*	
👤 *Username*	
✉ *Email*	
🔒 *Password*	
📝 *Note*	

	Website
👤	Username
✉	Email
🔒	Password
📝	Note

	Website
👤	Username
✉	Email
🔒	Password
📝	Note

	Website
👤	Username
✉	Email
🔒	Password
📝	Note

	Website
👤	Username
✉	Email
🔒	Password
📝	Note

🌐 Website	
👤 Username	
✉ Email	
🔒 Password	
📝 Note	

🌐 Website	
👤 Username	
✉ Email	
🔒 Password	
📝 Note	

🌐 Website	
👤 Username	
✉ Email	
🔒 Password	
📝 Note	

🌐 Website	
👤 Username	
✉ Email	
🔒 Password	
📝 Note	

🌐 Website	
👤 Username	
✉ Email	
🔒 Password	
📝 Note	

🌐 Website	
👤 Username	
✉ Email	
🔒 Password	
📝 Note	

🌐 Website	
👤 Username	
✉ Email	
🔒 Password	
📝 Note	

🌐 Website	
👤 Username	
✉ Email	
🔒 Password	
📝 Note	

<table>
<tr><td>**H**</td><td>Password Log Book</td><td>Date</td></tr>
</table>

🌐 Website	
👤 Username	
✉ Email	
🔒 Password	
📝 Note	

🌐 Website	
👤 Username	
✉ Email	
🔒 Password	
📝 Note	

🌐 Website	
👤 Username	
✉ Email	
🔒 Password	
📝 Note	

🌐 Website	
👤 Username	
✉ Email	
🔒 Password	
📝 Note	

🌐 Website	
👤 Username	
✉ Email	
🔒 Password	
📝 Note	

🌐 Website	
👤 Username	
✉ Email	
🔒 Password	
📝 Note	

🌐 Website	
👤 Username	
✉ Email	
🔒 Password	
📝 Note	

🌐 Website	
👤 Username	
✉ Email	
🔒 Password	
📝 Note	

🌐 Website	
👤 Username	
✉ Email	
🔒 Password	
📝 Note	

🌐 Website	
👤 Username	
✉ Email	
🔒 Password	
📝 Note	

🌐 Website	
👤 Username	
✉ Email	
🔒 Password	
📝 Note	

🌐 Website	
👤 Username	
✉ Email	
🔒 Password	
📝 Note	

🌐 Website	
👤 Username	
✉ Email	
🔒 Password	
📝 Note	

🌐 Website	
👤 Username	
✉ Email	
🔒 Password	
📝 Note	

🌐 Website	
👤 Username	
✉ Email	
🔒 Password	
📝 Note	

🌐 Website	
👤 Username	
✉ Email	
🔒 Password	
📝 Note	

I Password Log Book   Date

🌐 Website	
👤 Username	
✉ Email	
🔒 Password	
📝 Note	

🌐 Website	
👤 Username	
✉ Email	
🔒 Password	
📝 Note	

🌐 Website	
👤 Username	
✉ Email	
🔒 Password	
📝 Note	

🌐 Website	
👤 Username	
✉ Email	
🔒 Password	
📝 Note	

🌐 Website	
👤 Username	
✉ Email	
🔒 Password	
📝 Note	

🌐 Website	
👤 Username	
✉ Email	
🔒 Password	
📝 Note	

🌐 Website	
👤 Username	
✉ Email	
🔒 Password	
📝 Note	

🌐 Website	
👤 Username	
✉ Email	
🔒 Password	
📝 Note	

🌐 Website	
👤 Username	
✉ Email	
🔒 Password	
📝 Note	

🌐 Website	
👤 Username	
✉ Email	
🔒 Password	
📝 Note	

🌐 Website	
👤 Username	
✉ Email	
🔒 Password	
📝 Note	

🌐 Website	
👤 Username	
✉ Email	
🔒 Password	
📝 Note	

Password Log Book

Date

🌐 Website	
👤 Username	
✉ Email	
🔒 Password	
📝 Note	

🌐 Website	
👤 Username	
✉ Email	
🔒 Password	
📝 Note	

🌐 Website	
👤 Username	
✉ Email	
🔒 Password	
📝 Note	

🌐 Website	
👤 Username	
✉ Email	
🔒 Password	
📝 Note	

🌐 Website	
👤 Username	
✉ Email	
🔒 Password	
📝 Note	

🌐 Website	
👤 Username	
✉ Email	
🔒 Password	
📝 Note	

🌐 Website	
👤 Username	
✉ Email	
🔒 Password	
📝 Note	

🌐 Website	
👤 Username	
✉ Email	
🔒 Password	
📝 Note	

🌐 Website	
👤 Username	
✉ Email	
🔒 Password	
📝 Note	

🌐 Website	
👤 Username	
✉ Email	
🔒 Password	
📝 Note	

🌐 Website	
👤 Username	
✉ Email	
🔒 Password	
📝 Note	

🌐 Website	
👤 Username	
✉ Email	
🔒 Password	
📝 Note	

🌐 Website	
👤 Username	
✉ Email	
🔒 Password	
📝 Note	

🌐 Website	
👤 Username	
✉ Email	
🔒 Password	
📝 Note	

🌐 Website	
👤 Username	
✉ Email	
🔒 Password	
📝 Note	

🌐 Website	
👤 Username	
✉ Email	
🔒 Password	
📝 Note	

⊕ Website	
👤 Username	
✉ Email	
🔒 Password	
📝 Note	

⊕ Website	
👤 Username	
✉ Email	
🔒 Password	
📝 Note	

⊕ Website	
👤 Username	
✉ Email	
🔒 Password	
📝 Note	

⊕ Website	
👤 Username	
✉ Email	
🔒 Password	
📝 Note	

🌐 Website	
👤 Username	
✉ Email	
🔒 Password	
📝 Note	

🌐 Website	
👤 Username	
✉ Email	
🔒 Password	
📝 Note	

🌐 Website	
👤 Username	
✉ Email	
🔒 Password	
📝 Note	

🌐 Website	
👤 Username	
✉ Email	
🔒 Password	
📝 Note	

<table>
<tr><td>**K**</td><td>Password Log Book</td><td>Date</td></tr>
</table>

🌐 Website	
👤 Username	
✉ Email	
🔒 Password	
📝 Note	

🌐 Website	
👤 Username	
✉ Email	
🔒 Password	
📝 Note	

🌐 Website	
👤 Username	
✉ Email	
🔒 Password	
📝 Note	

🌐 Website	
👤 Username	
✉ Email	
🔒 Password	
📝 Note	

🌐 Website	
👤 Username	
✉ Email	
🔒 Password	
📝 Note	

🌐 Website	
👤 Username	
✉ Email	
🔒 Password	
📝 Note	

🌐 Website	
👤 Username	
✉ Email	
🔒 Password	
📝 Note	

🌐 Website	
👤 Username	
✉ Email	
🔒 Password	
📝 Note	

🌐 Website	
👤 Username	
✉ Email	
🔒 Password	
📝 Note	

🌐 Website	
👤 Username	
✉ Email	
🔒 Password	
📝 Note	

🌐 Website	
👤 Username	
✉ Email	
🔒 Password	
📝 Note	

🌐 Website	
👤 Username	
✉ Email	
🔒 Password	
📝 Note	

L Password Log Book   Date

Website	
Username	
Email	
Password	
Note	

Website	
Username	
Email	
Password	
Note	

Website	
Username	
Email	
Password	
Note	

Website	
Username	
Email	
Password	
Note	

🌐 Website	
👤 Username	
✉ Email	
🔒 Password	
📝 Note	

🌐 Website	
👤 Username	
✉ Email	
🔒 Password	
📝 Note	

🌐 Website	
👤 Username	
✉ Email	
🔒 Password	
📝 Note	

🌐 Website	
👤 Username	
✉ Email	
🔒 Password	
📝 Note	

🌐 Website	
👤 Username	
✉ Email	
🔒 Password	
📝 Note	

🌐 Website	
👤 Username	
✉ Email	
🔒 Password	
📝 Note	

🌐 Website	
👤 Username	
✉ Email	
🔒 Password	
📝 Note	

🌐 Website	
👤 Username	
✉ Email	
🔒 Password	
📝 Note	

🌐 Website	
👤 Username	
✉ Email	
🔒 Password	
📝 Note	

🌐 Website	
👤 Username	
✉ Email	
🔒 Password	
📝 Note	

🌐 Website	
👤 Username	
✉ Email	
🔒 Password	
📝 Note	

🌐 Website	
👤 Username	
✉ Email	
🔒 Password	
📝 Note	

🌐 Website	
👤 Username	
✉ Email	
🔒 Password	
📝 Note	

🌐 Website	
👤 Username	
✉ Email	
🔒 Password	
📝 Note	

🌐 Website	
👤 Username	
✉ Email	
🔒 Password	
📝 Note	

🌐 Website	
👤 Username	
✉ Email	
🔒 Password	
📝 Note	

🌐 Website	
👤 Username	
✉ Email	
🔒 Password	
📝 Note	

🌐 Website	
👤 Username	
✉ Email	
🔒 Password	
📝 Note	

🌐 Website	
👤 Username	
✉ Email	
🔒 Password	
📝 Note	

🌐 Website	
👤 Username	
✉ Email	
🔒 Password	
📝 Note	

🌐 Website	
👤 Username	
✉ Email	
🔒 Password	
📝 Note	

🌐 Website	
👤 Username	
✉ Email	
🔒 Password	
📝 Note	

🌐 Website	
👤 Username	
✉ Email	
🔒 Password	
📝 Note	

🌐 Website	
👤 Username	
✉ Email	
🔒 Password	
📝 Note	

🌐 Website	
👤 Username	
✉ Email	
🔒 Password	
📝 Note	

🌐 Website	
👤 Username	
✉ Email	
🔒 Password	
📝 Note	

🌐 Website	
👤 Username	
✉ Email	
🔒 Password	
📝 Note	

🌐 Website	
👤 Username	
✉ Email	
🔒 Password	
📝 Note	

Website	
Username	
Email	
Password	
Note	

Website	
Username	
Email	
Password	
Note	

Website	
Username	
Email	
Password	
Note	

Website	
Username	
Email	
Password	
Note	

🌐 *Website*	
👤 *Username*	
✉ *Email*	
🔒 *Password*	
📝 *Note*	

🌐 *Website*	
👤 *Username*	
✉ *Email*	
🔒 *Password*	
📝 *Note*	

🌐 *Website*	
👤 *Username*	
✉ *Email*	
🔒 *Password*	
📝 *Note*	

🌐 *Website*	
👤 *Username*	
✉ *Email*	
🔒 *Password*	
📝 *Note*	

🌐 *Website*	
👤 *Username*	
✉ *Email*	
🔒 *Password*	
📝 *Note*	

🌐 *Website*	
👤 *Username*	
✉ *Email*	
🔒 *Password*	
📝 *Note*	

🌐 *Website*	
👤 *Username*	
✉ *Email*	
🔒 *Password*	
📝 *Note*	

🌐 *Website*	
👤 *Username*	
✉ *Email*	
🔒 *Password*	
📝 *Note*	

🌐 Website	
👤 Username	
✉ Email	
🔒 Password	
📝 Note	

🌐 Website	
👤 Username	
✉ Email	
🔒 Password	
📝 Note	

🌐 Website	
👤 Username	
✉ Email	
🔒 Password	
📝 Note	

🌐 Website	
👤 Username	
✉ Email	
🔒 Password	
📝 Note	

🌐 Website	
👤 Username	
✉ Email	
🔒 Password	
📝 Note	

🌐 Website	
👤 Username	
✉ Email	
🔒 Password	
📝 Note	

🌐 Website	
👤 Username	
✉ Email	
🔒 Password	
📝 Note	

🌐 Website	
👤 Username	
✉ Email	
🔒 Password	
📝 Note	

🌐 Website	
👤 Username	
✉ Email	
🔒 Password	
📝 Note	

🌐 Website	
👤 Username	
✉ Email	
🔒 Password	
📝 Note	

🌐 Website	
👤 Username	
✉ Email	
🔒 Password	
📝 Note	

🌐 Website	
👤 Username	
✉ Email	
🔒 Password	
📝 Note	

🌐 Website	
👤 Username	
✉ Email	
🔒 Password	
📝 Note	

🌐 Website	
👤 Username	
✉ Email	
🔒 Password	
📝 Note	

🌐 Website	
👤 Username	
✉ Email	
🔒 Password	
📝 Note	

🌐 Website	
👤 Username	
✉ Email	
🔒 Password	
📝 Note	

Date

	Website	
	Username	
	Email	
	Password	
	Note	

	Website	
	Username	
	Email	
	Password	
	Note	

	Website	
	Username	
	Email	
	Password	
	Note	

	Website	
	Username	
	Email	
	Password	
	Note	

🌐 Website	
👤 Username	
✉ Email	
🔒 Password	
📝 Note	

🌐 Website	
👤 Username	
✉ Email	
🔒 Password	
📝 Note	

🌐 Website	
👤 Username	
✉ Email	
🔒 Password	
📝 Note	

🌐 Website	
👤 Username	
✉ Email	
🔒 Password	
📝 Note	

🌐 Website	
👤 Username	
✉ Email	
🔒 Password	
📝 Note	

🌐 Website	
👤 Username	
✉ Email	
🔒 Password	
📝 Note	

🌐 Website	
👤 Username	
✉ Email	
🔒 Password	
📝 Note	

🌐 Website	
👤 Username	
✉ Email	
🔒 Password	
📝 Note	

🌐 Website	
👤 Username	
✉ Email	
🔒 Password	
📝 Note	

🌐 Website	
👤 Username	
✉ Email	
🔒 Password	
📝 Note	

🌐 Website	
👤 Username	
✉ Email	
🔒 Password	
📝 Note	

🌐 Website	
👤 Username	
✉ Email	
🔒 Password	
📝 Note	

🌐 Website	
👤 Username	
✉ Email	
🔒 Password	
📝 Note	

🌐 Website	
👤 Username	
✉ Email	
🔒 Password	
📝 Note	

🌐 Website	
👤 Username	
✉ Email	
🔒 Password	
📝 Note	

🌐 Website	
👤 Username	
✉ Email	
🔒 Password	
📝 Note	

🌐 *Website*	
👤 *Username*	
✉ *Email*	
🔒 *Password*	
📝 *Note*	

🌐 *Website*	
👤 *Username*	
✉ *Email*	
🔒 *Password*	
📝 *Note*	

🌐 *Website*	
👤 *Username*	
✉ *Email*	
🔒 *Password*	
📝 *Note*	

🌐 *Website*	
👤 *Username*	
✉ *Email*	
🔒 *Password*	
📝 *Note*	

🌐 Website	
👤 Username	
✉ Email	
🔒 Password	
📝 Note	

🌐 Website	
👤 Username	
✉ Email	
🔒 Password	
📝 Note	

🌐 Website	
👤 Username	
✉ Email	
🔒 Password	
📝 Note	

🌐 Website	
👤 Username	
✉ Email	
🔒 Password	
📝 Note	

🌐 *Website*	
👤 *Username*	
✉ *Email*	
🔒 *Password*	
📝 *Note*	

🌐 *Website*	
👤 *Username*	
✉ *Email*	
🔒 *Password*	
📝 *Note*	

🌐 *Website*	
👤 *Username*	
✉ *Email*	
🔒 *Password*	
📝 *Note*	

🌐 *Website*	
👤 *Username*	
✉ *Email*	
🔒 *Password*	
📝 *Note*	

🌐 Website	
👤 Username	
✉ Email	
🔒 Password	
📝 Note	

🌐 Website	
👤 Username	
✉ Email	
🔒 Password	
📝 Note	

🌐 Website	
👤 Username	
✉ Email	
🔒 Password	
📝 Note	

🌐 Website	
👤 Username	
✉ Email	
🔒 Password	
📝 Note	

<table>
<tr><td>R</td><td>Password Log Book</td><td>Date</td></tr>
</table>

🌐 Website	
👤 Username	
✉ Email	
🔒 Password	
📝 Note	

🌐 Website	
👤 Username	
✉ Email	
🔒 Password	
📝 Note	

🌐 Website	
👤 Username	
✉ Email	
🔒 Password	
📝 Note	

🌐 Website	
👤 Username	
✉ Email	
🔒 Password	
📝 Note	

🌐 Website	
👤 Username	
✉️ Email	
🔒 Password	
📝 Note	

🌐 Website	
👤 Username	
✉️ Email	
🔒 Password	
📝 Note	

🌐 Website	
👤 Username	
✉️ Email	
🔒 Password	
📝 Note	

🌐 Website	
👤 Username	
✉️ Email	
🔒 Password	
📝 Note	

🌐 Website	
👤 Username	
✉ Email	
🔒 Password	
📝 Note	

🌐 Website	
👤 Username	
✉ Email	
🔒 Password	
📝 Note	

🌐 Website	
👤 Username	
✉ Email	
🔒 Password	
📝 Note	

🌐 Website	
👤 Username	
✉ Email	
🔒 Password	
📝 Note	

Website	
Username	
Email	
Password	
Note	

Website	
Username	
Email	
Password	
Note	

Website	
Username	
Email	
Password	
Note	

Website	
Username	
Email	
Password	
Note	

🌐 Website	
👤 Username	
✉ Email	
🔒 Password	
📝 Note	

🌐 Website	
👤 Username	
✉ Email	
🔒 Password	
📝 Note	

🌐 Website	
👤 Username	
✉ Email	
🔒 Password	
📝 Note	

🌐 Website	
👤 Username	
✉ Email	
🔒 Password	
📝 Note	

🌐 Website	
👤 Username	
✉ Email	
🔒 Password	
📝 Note	

🌐 Website	
👤 Username	
✉ Email	
🔒 Password	
📝 Note	

🌐 Website	
👤 Username	
✉ Email	
🔒 Password	
📝 Note	

🌐 Website	
👤 Username	
✉ Email	
🔒 Password	
📝 Note	

🌐 Website	
👤 Username	
✉ Email	
🔒 Password	
📝 Note	

🌐 Website	
👤 Username	
✉ Email	
🔒 Password	
📝 Note	

🌐 Website	
👤 Username	
✉ Email	
🔒 Password	
📝 Note	

🌐 Website	
👤 Username	
✉ Email	
🔒 Password	
📝 Note	

Password Log Book   Date

🌐 Website	
👤 Username	
✉ Email	
🔒 Password	
📝 Note	

🌐 Website	
👤 Username	
✉ Email	
🔒 Password	
📝 Note	

🌐 Website	
👤 Username	
✉ Email	
🔒 Password	
📝 Note	

🌐 Website	
👤 Username	
✉ Email	
🔒 Password	
📝 Note	

Website	
Username	
Email	
Password	
Note	

Website	
Username	
Email	
Password	
Note	

Website	
Username	
Email	
Password	
Note	

Website	
Username	
Email	
Password	
Note	

🌐 Website	
👤 Username	
✉ Email	
🔒 Password	
📝 Note	

🌐 Website	
👤 Username	
✉ Email	
🔒 Password	
📝 Note	

🌐 Website	
👤 Username	
✉ Email	
🔒 Password	
📝 Note	

🌐 Website	
👤 Username	
✉ Email	
🔒 Password	
📝 Note	

🌐 Website	
👤 Username	
✉ Email	
🔒 Password	
📝 Note	

🌐 Website	
👤 Username	
✉ Email	
🔒 Password	
📝 Note	

🌐 Website	
👤 Username	
✉ Email	
🔒 Password	
📝 Note	

🌐 Website	
👤 Username	
✉ Email	
🔒 Password	
📝 Note	

🌐 Website	
👤 Username	
✉ Email	
🔒 Password	
📝 Note	

🌐 Website	
👤 Username	
✉ Email	
🔒 Password	
📝 Note	

🌐 Website	
👤 Username	
✉ Email	
🔒 Password	
📝 Note	

🌐 Website	
👤 Username	
✉ Email	
🔒 Password	
📝 Note	

🌐 Website	
👤 Username	
✉ Email	
🔒 Password	
📝 Note	

🌐 Website	
👤 Username	
✉ Email	
🔒 Password	
📝 Note	

🌐 Website	
👤 Username	
✉ Email	
🔒 Password	
📝 Note	

🌐 Website	
👤 Username	
✉ Email	
🔒 Password	
📝 Note	

🌐 Website	
👤 Username	
✉ Email	
🔒 Password	
📝 Note	

🌐 Website	
👤 Username	
✉ Email	
🔒 Password	
📝 Note	

🌐 Website	
👤 Username	
✉ Email	
🔒 Password	
📝 Note	

🌐 Website	
👤 Username	
✉ Email	
🔒 Password	
📝 Note	

🌐 Website	
👤 Username	
✉ Email	
🔒 Password	
📝 Note	

🌐 Website	
👤 Username	
✉ Email	
🔒 Password	
📝 Note	

🌐 Website	
👤 Username	
✉ Email	
🔒 Password	
📝 Note	

🌐 Website	
👤 Username	
✉ Email	
🔒 Password	
📝 Note	

🌐 Website	
👤 Username	
✉ Email	
🔒 Password	
📝 Note	

🌐 Website	
👤 Username	
✉ Email	
🔒 Password	
📝 Note	

🌐 Website	
👤 Username	
✉ Email	
🔒 Password	
📝 Note	

🌐 Website	
👤 Username	
✉ Email	
🔒 Password	
📝 Note	

Password Log Book

<table>
<tr><td>V</td><td>Password Log Book</td><td>Date</td></tr>
</table>

🌐 Website	
👤 Username	
✉ Email	
🔒 Password	
📝 Note	

🌐 Website	
👤 Username	
✉ Email	
🔒 Password	
📝 Note	

🌐 Website	
👤 Username	
✉ Email	
🔒 Password	
📝 Note	

🌐 Website	
👤 Username	
✉ Email	
🔒 Password	
📝 Note	

🌐 Website	
👤 Username	
✉ Email	
🔒 Password	
📝 Note	

🌐 Website	
👤 Username	
✉ Email	
🔒 Password	
📝 Note	

🌐 Website	
👤 Username	
✉ Email	
🔒 Password	
📝 Note	

🌐 Website	
👤 Username	
✉ Email	
🔒 Password	
📝 Note	

<table>
<tr><td>**V**</td><td>Password Log Book</td><td>Date</td></tr>
</table>

🌐 Website	
👤 Username	
✉ Email	
🔒 Password	
📝 Note	

🌐 Website	
👤 Username	
✉ Email	
🔒 Password	
📝 Note	

🌐 Website	
👤 Username	
✉ Email	
🔒 Password	
📝 Note	

🌐 Website	
👤 Username	
✉ Email	
🔒 Password	
📝 Note	

🌐 Website	
👤 Username	
✉ Email	
🔒 Password	
📝 Note	

🌐 Website	
👤 Username	
✉ Email	
🔒 Password	
📝 Note	

🌐 Website	
👤 Username	
✉ Email	
🔒 Password	
📝 Note	

🌐 Website	
👤 Username	
✉ Email	
🔒 Password	
📝 Note	

🌐 Website	
👤 Username	
✉ Email	
🔒 Password	
📝 Note	

🌐 Website	
👤 Username	
✉ Email	
🔒 Password	
📝 Note	

🌐 Website	
👤 Username	
✉ Email	
🔒 Password	
📝 Note	

🌐 Website	
👤 Username	
✉ Email	
🔒 Password	
📝 Note	

🌐 *Website*	
👤 *Username*	
✉ *Email*	
🔒 *Password*	
📝 *Note*	

🌐 *Website*	
👤 *Username*	
✉ *Email*	
🔒 *Password*	
📝 *Note*	

🌐 *Website*	
👤 *Username*	
✉ *Email*	
🔒 *Password*	
📝 *Note*	

🌐 *Website*	
👤 *Username*	
✉ *Email*	
🔒 *Password*	
📝 *Note*	

🌐 Website	
👤 Username	
✉ Email	
🔒 Password	
📝 Note	

🌐 Website	
👤 Username	
✉ Email	
🔒 Password	
📝 Note	

🌐 Website	
👤 Username	
✉ Email	
🔒 Password	
📝 Note	

🌐 Website	
👤 Username	
✉ Email	
🔒 Password	
📝 Note	

🌐 Website	
👤 Username	
✉ Email	
🔒 Password	
📝 Note	

🌐 Website	
👤 Username	
✉ Email	
🔒 Password	
📝 Note	

🌐 Website	
👤 Username	
✉ Email	
🔒 Password	
📝 Note	

🌐 Website	
👤 Username	
✉ Email	
🔒 Password	
📝 Note	

🌐 Website	
👤 Username	
✉ Email	
🔒 Password	
📝 Note	

🌐 Website	
👤 Username	
✉ Email	
🔒 Password	
📝 Note	

🌐 Website	
👤 Username	
✉ Email	
🔒 Password	
📝 Note	

🌐 Website	
👤 Username	
✉ Email	
🔒 Password	
📝 Note	

🌐 Website	
👤 Username	
✉ Email	
🔒 Password	
📝 Note	

🌐 Website	
👤 Username	
✉ Email	
🔒 Password	
📝 Note	

🌐 Website	
👤 Username	
✉ Email	
🔒 Password	
📝 Note	

🌐 Website	
👤 Username	
✉ Email	
🔒 Password	
📝 Note	

<table>
<tr><td>X</td><td>Password Log Book</td><td>Date</td></tr>
</table>

🌐 Website	
👤 Username	
✉ Email	
🔒 Password	
📝 Note	

🌐 Website	
👤 Username	
✉ Email	
🔒 Password	
📝 Note	

🌐 Website	
👤 Username	
✉ Email	
🔒 Password	
📝 Note	

🌐 Website	
👤 Username	
✉ Email	
🔒 Password	
📝 Note	

🌐 Website	
👤 Username	
✉ Email	
🔒 Password	
📝 Note	

🌐 Website	
👤 Username	
✉ Email	
🔒 Password	
📝 Note	

🌐 Website	
👤 Username	
✉ Email	
🔒 Password	
📝 Note	

🌐 Website	
👤 Username	
✉ Email	
🔒 Password	
📝 Note	

🌐 Website	
👤 Username	
✉ Email	
🔒 Password	
📝 Note	

🌐 Website	
👤 Username	
✉ Email	
🔒 Password	
📝 Note	

🌐 Website	
👤 Username	
✉ Email	
🔒 Password	
📝 Note	

🌐 Website	
👤 Username	
✉ Email	
🔒 Password	
📝 Note	

🌐 Website	
👤 Username	
✉ Email	
🔒 Password	
📝 Note	

🌐 Website	
👤 Username	
✉ Email	
🔒 Password	
📝 Note	

🌐 Website	
👤 Username	
✉ Email	
🔒 Password	
📝 Note	

🌐 Website	
👤 Username	
✉ Email	
🔒 Password	
📝 Note	

🌐 *Website*	
👤 *Username*	
✉ *Email*	
🔒 *Password*	
📝 *Note*	

🌐 *Website*	
👤 *Username*	
✉ *Email*	
🔒 *Password*	
📝 *Note*	

🌐 *Website*	
👤 *Username*	
✉ *Email*	
🔒 *Password*	
📝 *Note*	

🌐 *Website*	
👤 *Username*	
✉ *Email*	
🔒 *Password*	
📝 *Note*	

🌐 Website	
👤 Username	
✉ Email	
🔒 Password	
📝 Note	

🌐 Website	
👤 Username	
✉ Email	
🔒 Password	
📝 Note	

🌐 Website	
👤 Username	
✉ Email	
🔒 Password	
📝 Note	

🌐 Website	
👤 Username	
✉ Email	
🔒 Password	
📝 Note	

🌐 Website	
👤 Username	
✉ Email	
🔒 Password	
📝 Note	

🌐 Website	
👤 Username	
✉ Email	
🔒 Password	
📝 Note	

🌐 Website	
👤 Username	
✉ Email	
🔒 Password	
📝 Note	

🌐 Website	
👤 Username	
✉ Email	
🔒 Password	
📝 Note	

🌐 Website	
👤 Username	
✉️ Email	
🔒 Password	
📝 Note	

🌐 Website	
👤 Username	
✉️ Email	
🔒 Password	
📝 Note	

🌐 Website	
👤 Username	
✉️ Email	
🔒 Password	
📝 Note	

🌐 Website	
👤 Username	
✉️ Email	
🔒 Password	
📝 Note	

🌐 Website	
👤 Username	
✉ Email	
🔒 Password	
📝 Note	

🌐 Website	
👤 Username	
✉ Email	
🔒 Password	
📝 Note	

🌐 Website	
👤 Username	
✉ Email	
🔒 Password	
📝 Note	

🌐 Website	
👤 Username	
✉ Email	
🔒 Password	
📝 Note	

	Website	
	Username	
	Email	
	Password	
	Note	

	Website	
	Username	
	Email	
	Password	
	Note	

	Website	
	Username	
	Email	
	Password	
	Note	

	Website	
	Username	
	Email	
	Password	
	Note